INTRODUCTION TO PODCASTING

LESSONS LEARNED
LESSONS SHARED

CONTENTS

Introduction
So you want to start a podcast?
Chapter 1: What are you going to talk about?   1
Chapter 2: What is in a name?   3
Chapter 3: What are you going to need?   5
Chapter 4: What time and what day(s)?   7
Chapter 5: What Platform should you use?   10
Chapter 6: What social media should you use?   13
Chapter 7: To interview or not to interview?   16
Chapter 8: The Final Countdown Chapter.   18

SO YOU WANT TO START A PODCAST?

But you don't know where or how to start or what tools you will need.

Don't worry I will share tips and tricks I have learned since starting my podcast and helping others start theirs.

Table of Contents

Chapter 1: What are you going to talk about?

Chapter 2: What is in a name?

Chapter 3: What are you going to need?

Chapter 4: What time and what day(s)?

Chapter 5: What Platform should you use?

Chapter 6: What social media should you use?

Chapter 7: To interview or not to interview?

Chapter 8: The Final Countdown.

CHAPTER 1: WHAT ARE YOU GOING TO TALK ABOUT?

So, what do you need first? Well the first thing is an idea for what to talk about. What is something that you are passionate about and like to talk about? There are over 500,000 active podcasts out there and there are so many varied subjects. So, you can really talk about anything.

Now with that many podcasts you may be thinking why bother or what if someone is already covering a subject that I want to talk about.

Well to quote Gary "Vee" Vaynerchuk

"With the ever-increasing value of speed, I am starting to see consumers replace entertainment (music) with information (podcasting) to get ahead."

More people than ever are listening to podcasts. So, this is really the way to go to get a message out there.

When I was starting out with writing and podcasting I always had this self-doubt that why would anyone want to listen to me. If that sounds familiar then let me share this that was told to me. No matter how many books or shows there are out there YOUR'S isn't.

So, don't let some silly self-talk stop you from going out there and following your dreams. Will you become a millionaire? Maybe,

maybe not, but the important part is to enjoy the journey.

So, what are you going to talk about?

CHAPTER 2: WHAT IS IN A NAME?

Okay so you have your subject matter now you need a name. You want something snappy and something that defines you and your subject matter. So, for instance if you were doing a show about oranges and how to grow and cultivate the perfect oranges for juice you could call your show Freshly Squeezed with Bob, if Bob is your name.

I know that is a silly name and example but you want it to let people know why you are there. You want them to see the name and stop and say to themselves. I wonder what this show is about then listen to it to find out.

You also want the shows name to be unique as well. So, what I recommend to anyone starting out is to go into iTunes and type in the name of the show you came up with. Once you see the search results you know if it is going to work.

You want to make it as easy as possible for people to find your show. So, you want to make sure yours is the only one that pops up. Some people don't bother with this and then there are 6 or 7 shows named the same thing and you have to figure it out.

One of my shows *The Creative Open Forum* is the only one named that. Now other shows will come up but mine is the only one with that name. So, you need something unique.

Now you may be thinking because I said open iTunes and search that you have to use Apple products or something like that. You don't but iTunes is the place where almost all podcasts are listed so it is the best place to search.

Now there is another reason you want a unique show name and that is SEO (Search Engine Optimization). If you have a show that shares a name with 6 other shows as you become more known it will be hard to find your show on Google too. I know people that have extremely popular shows with amazing guests and when you search the show on Google it isn't at the top nor is it close to the top. You want your show to be found.

So, I also recommend Googling your show title too just in case. Now I will provide some tips on how to increase your SEO as well later on. But for now, give your show a name and work with it to make sure you won't get lost in the crowd.

Now don't worry if things come up when you Google search. It will be fine you just don't want any podcasts to come up or other businesses that have the same name. So as long as you have few results that are exact or none you're okay because I'll teach you how to stack the deck in your favor.

So, come up with a name that is totally you and adjust it if needed to make it unique. Then you are a good way towards getting started.

CHAPTER 3: WHAT ARE YOU GOING TO NEED?

Well this is a simple question with potentially thousands of highly complicated answers.

Basically, at the end of the day all you really need is a smartphone or a tablet. You don't have to have a separate microphone.

Now that all of the podcasters that are reading this have come to after passing out from such sacrilege. To start you really only need that. Do I recommend a mic? Yes. But you can get away without it at first.

Now you can get fancy and record on your desktop or laptop with a microphone that cost several hundred dollars and do video recording to YouTube and all of that. Of Course, that is up to you. I wanted to learn more about recording before I jumped in at that level.

So when I first started recording shows I had my cell phone and the free headphones that came with it. It wasn't fancy but it got the job done. I was able to discover that I enjoyed Podcasting and then I started building up my gear bit by bit as I went.

Now I still use a wired set of headphones but you can use Bluetooth or even a more professional looking microphone. That is really up to you. I use a Logitech 390 USB gaming headset right now with an adapter to connect it to my phone.

But if you want to find out what other people are using you can check out https://kit.com. It is a site where people share what type of gear they use and their setups.

You can read reviews until you are blue in the face and still not know what you may want. But with this site you can see what other podcasters are using and that can give you an idea. Then you can listen to their show and see how it sounds to compare.

It is ok to take you time on this part and start out small. You want to make sure you get the right equipment for you and that it is compatible with how you want to use it. It saves you the time and trouble of returning stuff or spending more money than you need to.

CHAPTER 4: WHAT TIME AND WHAT DAY(S)?

So, your next order of business is the when of your show. Do you want to do a weekly show or a daily show? If weekly what day of the week and then what time do you want it to release?

Consistency is Key and so you want to make sure it is a schedule you can live with. Now you can schedule your episodes out on most of the platforms pretty easily. But you need a time to record your show when you will be able to work through it. Also, to do any edits if you are going to do that as well.

So, find a time that you can record and block it off. Or choose a time that you will not be distracted by others where you can't do much else. There are a couple podcasters I know of that record when they are driving. I also know of a few that have designated work from home days and they record when they are at home because they are closed off doing work anyways and they just throw on their headsets and record while they are typing.

You know it is whatever works for you but you want to make sure you are recording enough to be consistent. Once you start building a fan base they will expect their episodes to be released on time and if not, they may email you. It has happened to me before so I am speaking from experience.

The next thing to think about is when to release the episodes. I prefer to release mine early in the day so that if anyone is in on their commute to work. You could also post it right before the evening rush hour so that people can listen to it on the way home.

Keep in mind though that as Apple Podcast is one of the biggest platforms for listening try and gauge the time to make sure it is available there appropriately.

Originally my show would take about 2 hours to hit Apple after I submitted it via Anchor. Now it is closer to 30 - 45 minutes. So, if you want a show that is for that 5pm rush you might need to submit it around 3pm.

The next thing is daily vs weekly. It is a big commitment to do a daily show. Now you can always switch to a weekly format if you can't keep up with it. But it is up to you and how much time you can allot. There have been times where I have recorded several episodes in one day then scheduled them out.

Generally, for a daily show I recommend having a buffer of a couple extra shows in case you are sick or having technical difficulties. It never hurts to have a backup. I get up and record early so it isn't a problem but if you go on vacation for a week you might want to pre-record so you can enjoy your time away.

On a weekly show the biggest thing is what day. Now that can change based on what you are talking about. If you are doing a motivational show I would say Monday would be the best day. Most people in the work force are not fans of Mondays and so they need that pick me up. If you are doing a show about Fishing tips and tricks Saturday would be a good day because then you will have people listening on the weekend while they relax out on their boats fishing.

So find that balance and make the best choice for you. You can also research other shows that might be in the same niche as you and see what days their show airs too. Then schedule it on a day that their show isn't on. That way people can listen to you as well without giving up the time they dedicate to the other show.

Lastly you can always ask your friend or family. If they listen to podcasts you can ask them what days they prefer to hear a new show.

CHAPTER 5: WHAT PLATFORM SHOULD YOU USE?

So, there are a LOT of Podcast platforms. Each one has its advantages and disadvantages. But the trick is finding the one that you like the interface the most and that is a reasonable cost for you. I will list a couple and give you a rundown of some of the options and features

Chirp Micro Podcasting www.chirpapp.com
Chirp is a new platform and you could say it is the Twitter of Podcasting. You can only record a maximum of 2 minutes and you have a 140-character limit on your description. I find that it would be an ideal platform if you were wanting to do a podcast around quick tips like some of those 1-minute tip videos you see online.

The only major cons are that right now is that it is only available on iPhone and that it self-contained so people would either need the Chirp or be sent the show links via social media to listen on their browser.

Beyond that though it is a cool idea and I think it is taking flight just fine so far. I know that was a bad joke but I don't care.

Anchor www.anchor.fm

Anchor is the platform I use and I am very pleased with it. The app is available for both iOS and Android and you can either record from the App directly or import audio from any other source reasonably well.

It is 100% FREE and they even have an option that if you happen to be in New York you can book time to record in their studio and see what it is like to have that kind of a setup. On my next trip up, I am definitely doing that!

I have been running two podcasts on this platform for around 6 months and have had minimal issues but the scheduling is much easier to do from a computer. They are adding features all the time and I am sure they will clean that up but for now I record from my phone and upload it then I schedule the future date on my PC.

One thing they recently added was that you can have supporters that pledge monthly support like they would on Patreon and you can also record advertisements and make some residual income from that. You won't retire with the money but it will help pay for that gear that we talked about in Chapter 3.

As far as cons I would say one of the biggest gripes is that they publish out your show to all the major platforms and use their email address so you don't get the stats. However, to solve that issue, when you first setup your account there is a pop up that asks if you want them to do it for you and you can choose no. That means you submit everything and get those stat emails so problem solved there. The other support and I have not dealt with their support personally but a lot of people claim it is hard to get ahold of them.

There is an Anchor Facebook Group where there is really great community support and there are 3,100 members so that might be the best way to get help. Plus, every Thursday they have a thread where you can post a recent episode and I have actually gotten some listeners as a result.

Libsyn www.libsyn.com

This one I keep getting recommended by other podcasters. It seems to be an awesome platform with really great support overall. It is a pay platform that starts at $5 and goes up to $75 per month depending on the upload bandwidth you need.

The interesting thing to that is that the counter resets each month and your previous months uploads don't count against you. So, you don't have a storage limit per say just how many MB you upload each month. To me that seems very reasonable and perhaps one day I will make the switch.

You have the option to do advertisements and you have a bigger list of vendors to choose from since Libsyn is a larger and much older platform than Anchor. So that is a big plus if you are looking to monetize on a larger scale.

Really the only Con is the cost that I have ever heard. Not that this is a bad thing but if you are on a budget that might make platforms like this prohibitive. I chose Anchor as an option because I didn't know if I would stick with podcasting and didn't want to put a lot of money into it then have buyer's remorse.

Sound Cloud www.soundcloud.com

This is another great option and I know several people that podcast here. It is another pay option but unlike Libsyn you pay for the time. So, for free you get about 3 hours of time.

So, if you are recording 30 episodes you can record 6 podcast episodes then you are done unless you upgrade to the 6-hour plan or the unlimited plan. Personally, for podcasting the best option would be the Unlimited.

It is pretty easy to use from a PC, I have not tried it via the app. But all in all, it is a good platform and there are a lot of subscribers on Sound Cloud.

CHAPTER 6: WHAT SOCIAL MEDIA SHOULD YOU USE?

The simple answer is all of it. You want to probably setup a Facebook page, Twitter, Instagram, and possibly a website or blog.

You want everything to have similar names and a Logo that ties everything together. The App I used to create my logo was Canva initially which is available on iOS and Android. But some platforms have logo creators built in. But I prefer Canva over all.

So, get your Logo then start creating accounts. Now with Facebook and Twitter you can have banners so you can make those in Canva as well. It is an easy one stop shop for quick and convenient logo creation.

Twitter only allows 15-character names so I would start there and then work on the others. Like @tomsfunpodcast then use that for your Instagram and the URL for your Facebook (facebook.com/groups/tomsfunpodcast)

That way it is easy to get to and also it makes it easier when you are talking about it on the show to say find me at all these places just search tomsfunpodcast.

Now you may be busy and have a life, as well as other social media, and need to do some automation to help you advertise on these platforms. If so I have a solution for that.

If This Then That www.ifttt.com

If this then that is an IOT (Internet of Things) Automation site that is free to use. You can setup a couple hundred different things on top of auto posts for social media. Which that is what I use it for primarily. I setup tweets and posts reminding users to check out new episodes once a week. Even though I run a daily show I don't want to bombard them. Plus, I post real material also so it makes a nice compliment. It is super easy to setup and all you have to do is create your account and setup the accounts for the social media to allow access and then write up the posts.

They will post on the days you choose and then you are golden.

So, to give you an example you would choose the If This as "Date/Time" and Choose the day and time, obviously. Then the That would be Post a Tweet. It would then give you a box to type your message and then you save it and it does the rest.

SEO with FYI.to www.fyi.to

So, I promised SEO optimization and here it is. I use this site and it works beautifully and it is super easy to use. Basically, if you can Copy and Paste you are an expert already.

So, you would setup your account and then you are presented a link box. You copy all the links to your social media and the podcast one at a time into the box and it will make these cards.

Then you click create a smartlist it will then take you to the list. In the top right-hand corner of the screen you will see an edit button and then you can see an option to add tags to your list. Add as many as you can think of that are relevant. Like Podcast, podcaster, host, show, topic, interview, fishing.

Whatever you like to add then in the top left-hand side you will see the web address it will look something like this.

tomsfunpodcast.fyi.to/social-media-links-for-the-show

You can shorten the last part and Google likes short links to change it to
tomsfunpodcast.fyi.to/podcast

Then click save and you are all set. You can share this link out as the definitive way to find you and your show which is cool. But the best thing is that it increases your SEO rankings so your show starts moving up the list to be more easily found on search engines like Google and Bing.

The more easily you can be found the better!

CHAPTER 7: TO INTERVIEW OR NOT TO INTERVIEW?

So, should you interview people on your podcast? I would say yes and here is why. If you interview people they are going to talk about it to their friend and family and share it on social media. That helps you and your show reach people that you might not have reached otherwise. So, it is basically free publicity and advertising that you don't have to do a lot of work for.

There are several options to record interviews like Skype, Google Voice, Zoom, setting up a free conference line, etc. Then you can use a site like calendly.com to allow them to schedule a time with them and do the interview.

Also, equally important is the being interviewed. It helps you understand interviewing better and like the free publicity of getting people to interview you are sharing your story with a whole other audience that you might not have been able to reach otherwise.

So, it is also good to ask fellow podcasters to guest on your show and do crossover episodes. That works as well once you build up a relationship with them.

Lastly on this note your show will grow because you have people tuning in to hear you talk to these people and it will break up the show dynamic from sharing to interviewing and back.

I find it very helpful to keep me from getting into a rut as well.

CHAPTER 8: THE FINAL COUNTDOWN CHAPTER.

So one thing I offer and there is no cost involved is that if you want to try podcasting out and don't want to create all of this first just to see if it is something you would like to try I made *The Creative Open Forum* Podcast for that reason.

You can record some episodes and send them to me along with a show description for each to thecreativeopenforum@gmail.com

I will schedule them to be aired and you can listen to them and share them with your friends and family. I won't edit them or cut them to put ads in the middle or anything like that and that way you can see if you like it.

If you are good with that and want to continue you can create your show and you know you'll like doing it. Otherwise if you want them removed you can email me and I will take them down.

I started this because setting all this stuff up can be daunting and so I wanted to offer a try before you buy type of option for people and the show goes out to quite a few podcast channels Apple Podcasts, Anchor, Breaker, Castbox, Google Podcasts, Overcast, Pocket Casts, Radio Public, Spotify, and Stitcher. So, you'd get a pretty wide listening base for your test.

Check out More of my books here

Fiction
Hurtling Toward a Home: A Story of Hope

U.F.O.: What does that even mean?

The Journey Begins: Heroes or Monsters

Short Story
The Business of Earth: A future corporate owned world that has no history

Non-Fiction
Excuse me I don't think I have a box?

Random Writings of an Aspiring Writer: Stories from the road I am on.

So you want to start Podcasting

The Future of Retail: My thoughts on the future of Retail

Check out my Author page on Amazon
https://www.amazon.com/David-Calvert/e/B07LFM4BQB

www.ingramcontent.com/pod-product-compliance
Lightning Source LLC
Chambersburg PA
CBHW031511210526
45463CB00008B/3200